GHOSTS AND LEGENDS

OF NORTHUMBRIA

COQUET EDITIONS

First published in Great Britain in 1992.

This book incorporates some material first published in 'Ghosts &
Legends of Northumbria' and 'More Ghosts & Legends of
Northumbria' published in 1989 and the copyright of Sandhill Press.

© Coquet Editions
An imprint of Sandhill Press Ltd.
17 Castle Street, Warkworth,
Morpeth,
Northumberland, NE65 0UW

ISBN 0 946098 28 X

Ghosts & Legends of Northumbria: Selected and retold by
Hazel Reynolds and Editorial Staff at Sandhill Press.
Designed by Sandhill Press, set in Palatino 11pt.
Cover photograph *'Stone Hermit of Hulne Park'* © Sandhill Press.

'The Stone Hermit of Hulne Park', Alnwick, which guards the 'Nine Year
Aad Hole' dating from 1765, and featured on our front cover, is associated
with the following legend:
The statue guards a cave in which three robbers reputedly hid their chest of
stolen gold. One of the men went into Alnwick to buy food while the other
two dug a hole to bury the treasure. The two remaining men decided that
one should lie in wait for their companion and kill him, but as the
murderer, having completed the dirty deed, entered the cave he was stabbed
in the back by the remaining robber. Unfortunately he too later died as a
result of eating bread which had been poisoned by the first robber! The
treasure, alas, was never found!

Printed by St. Edmundsbury Press.

"From ghoulies and ghosties and long-leggety beasties
And things that go bump in the night,
Good Lord, deliver us!"

In former days nearly every village in Northumberland and
Durham possessed its own ghost, and people were very
respectful of them.
However, few people nowadays know how to approach a ghost
properly:
A spirit or ghost can not speak until it has been spoken to.
Speak slowly and clearly : "In the Name of the Father, Son and
Holy Ghost, who are you, and what is your business."

Whether you wait for a reply, is up to you...

CONTENTS

❖❖❖❖❖❖❖

The tiny island of Lindisfarne just off the North Northumberland coast has played an important part in the history of our region. Known also as Holy Island, it is renowned as the cradle of Christianity from the time of the missionary Aidan, who arrived there in 635 A.D. from Iona to begin his work of converting the Saxon people.

The most famous of the Bishops who succeeded Aidan was St. Cuthbert, who died in 687 A.D. at his retreat on Inner Farne, and was laid to rest at Lindisfarne until the monks were forced to flee in 875 A.D. The fact of the island being accessible from the mainland only twice a day at low tide adds to the mystery and romance which surrounds it. Sir Walter Scott described the setting in *'Marmion'*:

> *"For with the flow and ebb, its style*
> *Varies from continent to isle;*
> *Dry-shod, o'er sands, twice every day,*
> *The pilgrims to the shrine find way;*
> *Twice every day the waves efface*
> *Of staves and sandall'd feet the trace."*

In such a setting it is inevitable that there should be stories of strange happenings and hauntings, and of course, Holy Island's most famous ghost is St. Cuthbert himself. Perhaps it was because of his burial place being disturbed and his remains being moved by the monks to a greater place of safety, that his spirit still roams restlessly around Lindisfarne.

Certainly there have been many accounts of sightings of St. Cuthbert, and his ghost is said to regularly visit the abbey and parts of the island.

On dark, gloomy nights when the wind roars and the waves crash, the spirit of St. Cuthbert sits on the rocks near to Hobthrush. This is a basaltic peninsular of about half an acre, just east of Heugh Hill to the west of the harbour.

According to tradition Cuthbert works there, fashioning the famous 'Cuddy's Beads' into his rosary, the noise of his anvil echoing across the countryside. Again the poem *'Marmion'* provides an ideal account:

> *"On a rock by Lindisfarne*
> *St. Cuthbert sits, and toils to frame*
> *The sea-born beads that bear his name;*
> *Such tales had Whitby's fishers told,*
> *And said they might his shape behold,*
> *And hear his anvil sound;*
> *A deafening clang - a huge dim form*
> *Seen but, and heard, when gathering storm*
> *And night were closing round."*

The 'Cuddy's Beads' referred to are round button-like fossils, stems of encrinites or star-lilies sometimes to be found on the beach below Hobthrush, popularly called 'Feather-Stars' and considered locally as lucky charms.

St. Cuthbert's ghost also appears in the Priory and has been seen by choristers there. When Alfred the Great was a fugitive on Lindisfarne, he is supposed to have been assured by the same spirit that all would be well, and to have been told (correctly!) that he would one day be king of England.

The ghost monks are usually glimpsed in the area by the causeway which links the island to the mainland at low tide. These grey-clad figures are believed to be the spirits of the monks slaughtered in the Viking raids of 793 A.D., and they watch, even now, in trepidation for the heathen raiders' return.

THE LAIDLEY WORM OF SPINDLESTON

❖❖❖❖❖❖❖

The famous legend of the 'loathsome dragon' of Spindleston Heugh, near Bamburgh Castle, was printed in ballad verse in Hutchinson's 'Northumberland'. The Rev. Robert Lambe, Vicar of Norham, claimed to have transcribed it from a very old manuscript, and that the legend originated in a song *"made by the old mountain-bard, Duncan Frasier, living on the Cheviot about 1270."* Although this was discounted later, the story in various forms has survived, and remains one of the most well-known about Northumberland.

It relates that a Princess called Margaret, was living a lonely life in the huge fortress castle of Bamburgh. Her mother was dead, her brother away seeking fame and fortune, and her father, after years of mourning his first love, had travelled south in search of a new wife. News reached Bamburgh eventually that the King was returning with a new bride. Amid great excitement, a huge feast of welcome was prepared, and the whole village of Bamburgh turned out to welcome them.

The new Queen was tall and beautiful, but had been bewitched in childhood, and was in fact, evil and cold-hearted. She was instantly jealous of the lovely and popular Princess Margaret, and uttering a dreadful curse, she swore to turn her step-daughter into a 'laidley worm'. Only the return of Margaret's brother, the Prince, would release the innocent girl from the spell.

The Princess laughed aloud at these threats, but her heart missed a beat and she began to feel afraid as she looked into her Stepmother's cold and evil eyes. However, ignoring her feelings, Margaret retired peacefully to sleep.

But in the darkness of the night the evil magic began to

work. Next morning the girl had vanished - in her place hissed a venomous beast.

The old ballad tells that the 'Laidley Worm' crawled away from the castle and hid among some nearby caves, so terrorising the local population that:

"For seven miles east and seven miles west,
and seven miles north and south,
No blade of grass or corn could grow
So venomous was her mouth

The milk of seven streakit cows,
It was their cost to keep;
They brought her dayly, whyche she drank
Before she wente to sleepe"

This milk was taken to a large stone trough near the entrance of the cave where the dragon hid. Until recent times the cave and trough could still be seen at Spindleston, but their remains were destroyed in the nineteenth century by the opening of a quarry - and now only the Spindle Stone is standing. It is here that the hero of the ballad is said to have tethered his horse as he approached the worm's 'den'.

News of these dreadful events quickly spread and eventually reached the ears of Margaret's brother the Prince : 'The Childe of the Wynd'. Wild with grief and rage, he vowed a terrible revenge on his wicked Stepmother and immediately set sail for Bamburgh. As proof against her witchcraft his ship was constructed of rowanwood, which has the power to repel evil spirits.

The Prince had forgotten, however, the danger from the 'Laidley Worm' whose enormous tail lashed the waves into such a rough sea that the ship had to put about, and changed course to land at Budle Bay. As the Prince jumped from the ship, the dragon rose above the cliffs to meet him. It was a terrifying sight, breathing fire through its huge nostrils and whipping the sand dunes into a dust storm by the might of its breath.

Raising his sword to strike it down, the Prince heard these words:

> *"O quit thy sword and bend thy bow,*
> *And give me kisses three,*
> *For though I am a poisonous worm,*
> *No hurt I'll do to thee"*

Bravely of course, the prince did as he was asked, and immediately the dragon vanished! - and there instead stood his lovely sister Margaret.

Happily reunited, brother and sister set out in triumph for Bamburgh Castle. Here they confronted their evil Stepmother, who vainly entreated them to show her mercy. The Prince, though brave, honest and kindhearted, could not forgive the dreadful curse which she had inflicted on his beloved sister. In revenge he condemned the cruel Queen to: *"squat, crawl, hiss and spit in likeness of an ugly toad."*

As he said the words, the Queen disappeared and in her place hissed a huge and venomous toad. Chased from the castle the creature took refuge at the bottom of the castle well from which, the legend tells, she emerges from time to time to scare the unlucky passer-by!

> *"And on the land near Ida's towers*
> *A loathsome toad she crawls,*
> *And venom spits on everything*
> *That cometh nigh the walls."*

❖❖❖❖❖❖❖

It was a stormy, winter's night in Northumberland, the ruins of Dunstanburgh Castle stood proud on the rocks above the wild, crashing sea. Rain lashed at the remaining castle walls as the lightnings' flash illuminated the hollow towers. No trees or flowers grew there apart from one single yew tree, its branches bowed down under the howling gale. To this wild, untamed landscape came the gallant knight, Sir Guy, hoping to find shelter from the torrential rain. All the gates were barred against him, and he was forced to seek refuge in the porch to wait for the storm to clear.

Sir Guy, huddled against the lashing wind, watched the storm rage on relentlessly for about two hours until suddenly, at midnight, the castle doors burst open and a figure, surrounded by flames, appeared. There stood an old man, enormous in height, with a long, flowing white beard, and dressed in a dark, billowing robe tied at the waist by a burning hot chain. In his hand gleamed a wand of burning iron, and as he beckoned the brave knight into the castle, he cried:

> *"Sir Knight, Sir Knight! If your heart be right,*
> *And your nerves be firm and true,*
> *Sir Knight, Sir Knight! A beauty bright*
> *Indurance waits for you."*

Having passed through a labyrinth of passages filled with eerie sounds and creatures, they finally reached a solid brass door which, when opened, revealed a dimly lit hall. At least a hundred deathly pale, sleeping knights, guarded by their slumbering horses, lay in the hall.

*"Of marble black as the raven's back,
A hundred steeds stood round,
And of marble white by each a knight
Lay sleeping on the ground."*

Raised high up at the far end of the hall was a crystal tomb guarded by two enormous skeletons; one holding a sword, the other a horn. A beautiful young girl lay sleeping in the tomb bound by Merlin's spell which could only be broken by a 'valiant knight', brave enough to encounter the supernatural forces of the castle, and make the correct choice between the sword or the horn.

After careful consideration, Sir Guy chose the horn from the skeleton's grip. As he blew, the sound echoed and reverberated around the hall and the whole scene came to life. The knights awoke and the horses stamped their feet, as the girl raised her head in hope, but Sir Guy had made the wrong choice.

*"Now shame on the coward who sounded a horn
When he might have unsheathed a sword."*

Loud, scornful laughter filled the hall and a strange evil-smelling odour permeated the air, as the hall was plunged into darkness. Sir Guy collapsed unconscious and later found himself lying back in the porch, as dawn approached. Remembering his failure to rescue the girl, he searched the ruined castle to find the enchanted hall. Indeed, it is said he continued his search until he died and was buried in a nearby churchyard.

The legend relates that he continues to search after death, Merlin's spell still unbroken. The pale-red and yellow quartz crystals which can be found among the Dunstanburgh rocks are known as the 'Dunstanburgh Diamonds' and would have formed part of the treasure due to him, had Sir Guy succeeded in breaking the wizard's spell.

❖❖❖❖❖❖❖

Anyone who has visited Chillingham Castle, about 5 miles from Wooler, in North Northumberland, would not be surprised to hear that it is haunted. Dating originally from Norman times, and recently rescued from ruin by Sir Humphrey Wakefield, the castle consists of four huge towers which dominate a central courtyard, and visitors cannot fail to sense the brooding though romantic atmosphere which surrounds the building.

One strange incident happened at the turn of the century when some stones fell from the wall in a bedroom and in the cavity stood two 'grinning' skeletons, the bones of a man and a child. Could they have been the remains of enemies captured in a Border raid? Other bones were discovered in one of the dungeons and workmen were terrified to see a seated figure which appeared to be perfectly preserved, but crumbled to dust as the air rushed in. The dungeon walls bear the scratched lines and initials of prisoners captured during the Border Wars and who knows if their ghosts still linger in the dank, gloomy vaults?

A more well-known ghost is that of Lady Mary Berkeley, the wife of Ford, Lord Grey of Wark and Chillingham and Earl of Tankerville. *(The ancient Grey family captured Chillingham Castle and became the owners in the 12th century, later becoming known as the Tankervilles.)* Lady Mary is believed to be searching for her husband who ran away with his wife's sister, Lady Henrietta. This resulted in a huge scandal and a law suit conducted before the famous Judge Jeffries during the reign of Charles II.

The unfortunate lady was left alone at the castle with only her fatherless child for company and to this day the silky rustle of her dress is heard as the tragic figure moves along the corridors and on the stairs searching for her faithless husband.

The most famous apparition at Chillingham, however, was that of the 'Radiant Boy', said to have haunted what is now the Pink Room. The origins of this ghost were unknown at first, but on many occasions, as the clock struck midnight, terrible cries and the moans of a child in pain and fear could be heard coming from a place near to a passage which had been cut through the ten feet thick wall, into the adjoining tower. The heart rending cries would slowly die away as a bright halo of light appeared close to the four poster bed. Anyone sleeping there saw the figure of a boy dressed in blue and surrounded by light, approaching them.

In later years the bones of young boy and fragments of a blue dress were discovered in the wall. Once the remains were removed and given a decent burial the hauntings ceased.

Sir Humphrey Wakefield, who is related to the Greys by his third marriage, and is currently restoring the castle, has related how his son Maximilian, whilst staying alone at the castle, heard footsteps coming up the stairs towards his room, through the door and then through the wall.

Some time after this Sir Humphrey visited America on business and during his stay he consulted an Indian fortune teller. She suggested that Chillingham was not a safe place for his youngest son Jack, a child from his third marriage and thus a member of the Grey family. On his return to Northumberland, Sir Humphrey decided to have the castle exorcised - just in case...

❖❖❖❖❖❖❖❖

There are several versions of the legend which explain the existence of the lonely Hermitage on the banks of the River Coquet beside Warkworth Castle. Events began, it is generally agreed, at a banquet held in Alnwick Castle. Among the honoured guests was the Lord of Widdrington and his lovely daughter Isabel. She was loved by Sir Bertram of Bothal, one of the Earl Percy's knights. As was the custom of the time, Sir Bertram promised Isabel at this feast, that he would perform some deed of great daring to be worthy of marrying her.

The chance came when Earl Percy led his knights into Scotland to attack his hated enemy, the Earl Douglas. A fierce and bloody battle took place in which Sir Bertram fought very courageously. Unfortunately he was badly wounded when a Scottish sword struck his helmet from his head. Carried gravely injured to Wark Castle, he asked that a message be sent to Isabel begging her to come to his side.

During the long weeks of his recovery, Sir Bertram waited in vain for Isabel to arrive. As soon as he was able to ride, he set out with his brother to Isabel's home. On their arrival they were dismayed to learn that Isabel had left to travel to Wark immediately she received the message, and her family believed she was safely there.

Realising that Isabel must have been ambushed and kidnapped, a huge search was organised to find her. Sir Bertram and his brother decided to separate, and set off in different directions to help. Wandering through the countryside, often disguised as a minstrel or servant, Sir Bertram tried to find news of his lost love. At last he heard from a travelling monk about a beautiful princess held captive in the tower of a remote castle.

As this was the home of a Scottish chieftain who had long admired Isabel, Sir Bertram felt sure that at last he had the news for which he had so desperately sought. He set off at once for the place the monk had described, but when he reached the castle after a long and tiring journey, he was unable to gain admittance. He therefore sheltered in a nearby cave and kept watch. Eventually he was rewarded by the sight of Isabel framed in the window of the tower.

Relieved to have finally found her, Sir Bertram fell into an exhausted sleep. Awoken by strange noises, to his horror he saw Isabel being helped down a rope ladder and then onto a horse, by a figure in Highland costume. Assuming it to be one of his hated Scottish enemies, Sir Bertram leapt to his feet and, brandishing his sword, ran to the attack. Yelling, *"Die, traitor, Die - Let my Lady go"* he dealt his opponent a terrible blow and knocked him to the ground.

The terrified Isabel, recognising Sir Bertram's voice, rushed between the two men shrieking, *"Stop, Wait, its your own brother."* But it was too late. The next huge blow from Bertram's sword killed them both. Paralysed with grief and remorse Bertram lay as dead on the ground beside their bodies.

Eventually recovering at least physically from these dreadful events, Bertram gave all his lands and wealth away to the poor. With the permission of the Earl Percy he built with his own hands the tiny Hermitage beside the River Coquet, where he lived in solitude for the rest of his life.

The Hermitage consists of a tiny chapel, dormitory and cell. In the chapel is an altar - tomb on which lies the effigy of a beautiful lady, supposedly the Lady Isabel, her hands raised in prayer. At her feet kneels the figure of a hermit, his left hand pressed to his heart, as if in sorrow. The whole story is summed up by the inscription over the doorway, which translated reads: *"my tears have been my meat night and day"*

❖❖❖❖❖❖❖

This is a powerful tale of love triumphing over death itself. Set in Bedlington, near Blyth in Northumberland, it concerns a very rich but mean-natured couple whose only daughter was so beautiful *"with ruby lips and auburn hair"* that she was called 'The Flower of Bedlington'. She was deeply in love and loved by a worthy young man, James Robson, known for his goodness and *"generous acts and constant truth."* But although he was sober, steady, hard working and well-mannered, he was desperately poor, living in a meagre hovel and employed as a ploughman.

The girl's parents would have nothing to do with the young man and did all they could to break their daughter's attachment to him. They were resolved that she should marry a rich man of their choosing. In vain did they contrive all manner of tricks to keep the young couple apart, nothing had any effect. Finally in exasperation, they arranged to send their daughter to her uncle's farm at Stokesley in North Yorkshire. This was far enough away they felt to break the bond between the lovers.

During an anguished and tearful farewell the couple vowed their everlasting love for each other and the girl pledged:

> *"of love and truth through life sincere;*
> *nor death should part,*
> *for from the grave*
> *short time should the survivor save."*

Devastated by the separation, in less than a week, James fell dreadfully ill so that *"he sickened sore, and heart-broke died."*

16

This unhappy event delighted the girl's parents who determined to wed her at once to the wealthy suitor they had chosen. Almost before the unfortunate James was buried they made their preparations to travel to Stokesley and bring their daughter home for her marriage. They retired early to bed intending to set out very early the next day.

As midnight struck, the hour when *"restless ghosts their wrongs deplore"*, the newly deceased ploughman rode up to the farm at Stokesley to meet his love, mounted on her father's favourite horse. He knocked loudly at the door and when the girl called out to him he replied *"Come quick love. Here is your mother's cloak and hood and your father's good grey mare. You are to ride home with me at once."*

The girl rushed out to him, followed by her uncle who was rather disturbed by these events. However, when he saw James on the horse he recognised, with the clothes for the girl from her mother, he let them go with his blessing, although he made the young man swear to take his niece straight home *"without insult or injury, doubt or damage."*

No sooner was she seated up on the horse behind him, with her arm around his waist, than off they sped:

> *"They travelled faster than the wind;*
> *And in two hours, or little more,*
> *They came unto her father's door."*

During this headlong ride, James complained that his head was aching and the girl bound her own scarf around him. As she did so she cried *"My dear, you are as cold as lead."* Then as the moon broke from under a dark cloud, she noticed that he cast no shadow, unlike herself and the horse. Before she had time to realise the significance of this they had arrived at her home and James lifted her gently down from the horse.

"Your mare has travelled far;
So go you in, and, as I'm able
I'll feed and tend her in your stable."

Joyfully she knocked at the door of her house, calling to her parents that she was safely home with James. Surely, she thought, they must have changed their minds towards him to have sent him to bring her home.

Her father, hearing her words, shook with fright, knowing of course that James was dead and buried only that same day. Rushing from the house, he hurried to the stable to see who was there, but he could only find his own horse steaming with sweat from the long ride.

Back indoors the mother broke the dreadful news to her daughter, who, with a single cry, fell to the floor in a deep faint. The colour had all drained from her face, and her whole body trembled and shook as though in a fit.

Taken to her bedroom, she lay still and white on her bed, slowly and surely her life was ebbing from her. Frantically her parents brought the best doctors in the area to treat her, but all was in vain. They could find no physical cause for her condition, and shook their heads sadly, it was clear that she was rapidly fading away.

In a few short days she was dead. She only spoke to request that she be buried with James in the same coffin and grave. Her grief-stricken parents, now filled with remorse, prepared to do as she wished.

Strange to relate, when the coffin was opened, the girl's scarf was found tied around James' head, just as she had told her parents had happened on her ride home.

❖❖❖❖❖❖❖

Imagine an apparition dressed all in black, and hear the ghostly rustle of satin or silk as the mischievous 'Silky' glides around the houses or countryside of Northumbria...

There are several stories told about this strange supernatural being, known as Silky, because of the rustle of her skirts, many of them originating in the area of Belsay and Black Heddon.

The Silky of Belsay, near Morpeth, haunted the woods, lonely lanes and isolated farms, rather than one particular house. She delighted in appearing in one of these places and startling unsuspecting peasants, milk maids and horsemen. She would also wander to a lake at the bottom of Belsay Craig, and sit in a tree above the waterfall at the outlet to the lake. The tree became known as ' Silky's Chair', where, in her solitary moments, she enjoyed the sound of a storm through the trees and the crashing of the waters below.

In her behaviour, Silky bore a striking resemblance to the 'brownies', impish sprites who took delight in playing tricks on people. She always performed these at night between dark and dawn, and if people cleaned their houses on a Saturday ready for the Sabbath, Silky would disrupt everything and create confusion. Alternatively, if they were left untidy, everything would be put in order.

At the end of the eighteenth century, in the quiet village of Black Heddon, near Stamfordham, the local people were annoyed by the pranks of a mischievous apparition in rustling skirts. At night, on the lonely roads near Black Heddon, Silky would appear in front of the lone horsemen, or even, unexpectedly, sit behind them on their mounts. After enjoying a comfortable ride, she would dissolve away into the night, leaving behind a terrified and bewildered horse and rider.

She could also cause horses to be restless, and no amount of soothing or whipping would restrain them. The power of the rowan tree was the only thing that could deter Silky.

One night a farm worker had to go to a colliery for coal, and returning late to a farm near Black Heddon, the driver was waylaid by Silky at a bridge south of the village, known as 'Silky's Bridge'. As they arrived at the bridge, the horses suddenly stood absolutely still and would not, indeed, could not, move. The spell was finally broken when a neighbour brought some 'witch wood' or rowan tree, up to the horses. Snorting and blowing through their nostrils, they flicked their tails and moved on.

A Silky is also said to have haunted Denton Hall, a mansion to the west of Newcastle, on the Carlisle road. The 'rustling' ghost was said to haunt two rooms of the Hall in particular, and was often seen descending the stairs. Inhabitants of the Hall would hear heavy objects apparently being dragged around in an upstairs room, but on investigation, nothing had been disturbed.

During the latter part of the eighteenth century, when Denton Hall was owned by Mrs. Elizabeth Montagu, many famous people stayed as her guests including Dr. Johnson, Goldsmith, Garrick and Sir Joshua Reynolds. It was visitors to the Hall that Silky delighted in scaring, rather than the owners. In the *'Monthly Chronicles'*, it is the late Sir Thomas Doubleday who relates one such incident.

A wealthy fashionable young lady was staying at Denton Hall and had attended a ball at the Old Assembly Rooms in Newcastle. At the ball she had met, and fallen in love at first sight, with a handsome gentleman.

Returning to the Hall, she was sitting in her room at the dressing table musing on the evening's events, when she saw the figure of an old lady dressed in a flowered satin gown, seated in an antique chair by the fireplace. Huge rings flashed on her gnarled fingers, and over her head she wore a type of hood or mantilla, beneath which her face was criss-crossed with the wrinkles of old age.

The strange intruder spoke to the girl: *"So, my young lady, you've been at yon ball tonight and you've been highly delighted, I can see. But if you knew what I know and could see with my eyes, your pleasure would be less."* The old lady then began to deliver a lecture on the dangers of youth and the wicked ways of the times, denouncing the age as one of *"pride and poverty"* and *"It is an age of glitter and gloss like the pearl in your hair."* At the mention of the pearl, the young girl looked instinctively into the dressing table mirror, but when she turned back to face the woman, the room was empty. Although she could hear the rustle of silk and footsteps treading to the door, she could see no one.

Terrified, the girl lay awake for the remainder of the night, telling her hosts of her experience in the morning. They listened sympathetically, explaining that she was not the first visitor to have this uncanny encounter with Silky.

Silky disappeared from her various haunts very suddenly and an incident at a house at Black Heddon was thought to provide the explanation.

A maid, alone in one of the rooms of the house, was terrified when a ceiling suddenly crashed to the floor, bringing with it a black bundle covered with cobwebs. Believing this to be the devil's work, she fled from the house, screaming in terror. When the family inspected the bundle, it turned out to be a dog or calf's skin filled with gold treasure.

As Silky was not seen after this incident, it was popularly believed that she had been the restless phantom of the owner of the gold which had been lost, but her search now at an end, Silky could rest in peace.

❖❖❖❖❖❖❖

The legendary Meg o' Meldon was said to have been Margaret Selby, the daughter of a Newcastle money lender, William Selby. She most certainly inherited her father's miserly nature and greed for money. Reputedly not very attractive, she married Sir William Fenwick of Wallington, who may have been more interested in her financial circumstances rather than her physical attributes. Included in her dowry was a mortgage on Meldon Hall, then the inheritance of Heron, a good looking, fun-loving young man.

Sir William died many years before Margaret and his effigy still stands in Meldon church. Following his death, Meg foreclosed the mortgage on Meldon and set about running the estates and property herself. She proved to be an able farmer, gathering in good crops and attending market. She subsequently acquired large sums of money, revealing her avaricious nature, and began hoarding her wealth in many secret places.

By now she was spending most of her time at Hartington Hall, near Rothley. She is reported to have had an underground carriageway constructed between Hartington and Meldon, so that she could travel between the two unobserved. The more riches she obtained, the more she was compelled to hide them away, continually searching for new hiding places.

When Meg finally passed away, she was buried at Newminster Abbey, where her ghost was to be seen sitting on a stone trough, known as the 'Trough of the Maid of Meldon', by the archway in the graveyard. Her ghost was doomed to wander for seven years in search of the hoarded wealth, resting for seven years before continuing its quest. Local people also claimed to have seen her crossing Meldon Bridge in the shape of a black dog, changing into a beautiful woman at the other side.

One of Meg's hiding places was a deep draw-well on the Meldon Estate, where she had hidden gold wrapped in a bullock's hide and dropped it deep into the well. Her ghost was often seen mournfully gazing down into the well to seek her lost treasure.

One night a peasant worker on the estate had a strange dream, instructing him to search for the hidden riches. As a condition of his finding the gold, silence was to be maintained throughout the search. Being desperately poor, he accepted the challenge and took chains and a grappling hook to the well one night at midnight.

A mysterious figure was waiting for him, and silently it helped lower him into the well and retrieve the gold. The package was finally brought to the surface, but upon seeing the gold shining before his eyes, excitement prevailed and the peasant cried out: *"There! All the demons alive can't help me getting it now!"* The hooks released the glistening hoard, sending it back down into the depths of the well, never to be found again.

The old schoolhouse at Meldon was to be the scene of Meg's next revelation. Before her death, Meg had smuggled gold into the rafters of the old school, then a fairly strong, substantial building. However, having seen years of excited schoolboys playing and romping within its walls, the plaster was weakening and it could conceal its treasure no longer. One day, after dinner, the boys were engaged in their usual boisterous behaviour when suddenly the ceiling collapsed. After the dust settled, the boys scrambled for a share of the treasure.

Finally, when all her hiding places were revealed, and the hoards of wealth distributed, Meg was at last able to find peace.

THE LONG PACK

❖❖❖❖❖❖❖

The story of the Long Pack, concerning an attempted robbery at a rich gentleman's house on the North Tyne, is attributed to James Hogg, commonly known as the 'Ettrick Shepherd'. Hogg was a widely talented man who could write a story, poem or ballad equally well, and the Long Pack is a fine example of his ability to create vivid characters.

The country seat, which is the scene of these extraordinary events, is not actually named by Hogg but is widely believed to have been Chipchase, La Lee Hall or Swinburne. Chipchase and La Lee Hall are still inhabited but Swinburne fell into disrepair. Swinburne was, in fact, the most likely, although no Ridley ever lived there, but a family called Riddell did occupy it before and after these events took place.

Hogg tells us that in 1723 Colonel Ridley returned from India a rich man and retired to a country house on the banks of the North Tyne. It was said to be renovated and richly furnished containing a fine collection of silver and valuable goods. Colonel Ridley and his family, together with the majority of their servants, spent the winter months at their London home, leaving a skeleton staff at the country house. Three servants remained on this particular occasion : Alice, a maid servant; Richard, an old man who threshed the corn and Edward, who took care of the cattle.

On a cold, stormy winter's night, Alice was spinning yarn when a pedlar arrived at the Hall, with an enormous long pack on his shoulders. A pedlar was a common sight in those days and usually a welcome visitor, bringing news and gossip from other places.

This particular pedlar was a handsome man, flattering Alice and flirting with her. However, when he asked if he could stay overnight, he was refused. No amount of persuasion or bribery would induce Alice to change her mind, she had orders not to allow strangers to stay at the house.

The man conceded convincingly and asked if he could leave his pack overnight while he looked for shelter elsewhere. Alice agreed reluctantly and the pack was taken to a downstairs room, and placed carefully on two chairs. Alice was puzzled by the extreme length and weight of the pack, and could not help regarding it with suspicion. As she lit more candles, she was sure that the pack moved.

"Every hair on her head stood upright. Every inch of flesh on her body crept like a nest of pismires" (ants)

Alice fled through the kitchen and out into the barn in search of Richard. In an obviously agitated state she related the story to him, although he was reluctant to believe the idea of a 'living' pack. As they were standing over the pack discussing the situation, Edward entered with his old military gun he used for shooting - without success - birds who flew around the cattle fodder. Hogg gives the gun the splendid name of 'Copenhagen'.

Hearing the story, Edward was eager to use the gun on the pack but was restrained by Alice and Richard. However, when he thought he saw the pack move, he fired and was horrified to hear moans and groans as blood gushed out onto the floor. Bravely, the three of them opened the pack to reveal a dead man who had been carefully concealed inside two wooden boxes, a cutlass in his hand ready to cut his way out at the right moment. He also had four pistols hidden around him and a whistle to summon his accomplices. The servants quickly realised the plot to rob the house, and that the dead man's fellow thieves would be returning to await his signal.

They immediately alerted all the local help they could and armed them with a variety of weapons including the four pistols. Edward sounded the signal, which was answered, and within five minutes the sound of horses heralded the arrival of the accomplices. Edward fired the first shot, unable to contain himself, and there followed a volley of fire from the others, strategically placed at the windows of the house. They saw several men fall from their horses, their cries and moans echoing in the night. As the others retreated, Edward and another man went out to see what damage had been done. They found four bodies, but decided to leave them until daylight. However, the dawn revealed that the bodies had vanished : the other culprits had come to reclaim their dead, only *"large sheets of frozen blood"* showed where the bodies had lain.

News of the attack spread quickly as people came to gaze at the crimson stains on the frozen earth. It took a little longer to inform the Colonel of these events and he arrived five days later. A thorough search was made, but none of the culprits could be traced, and no clues were found as to the leader of the gang. The body found in the pack was kept for a fortnight but remained unrecognised and the Colonel finally had it buried at Bellingham. It was reported, however, that the grave was opened and the corpse removed.

The three servants were rewarded for their bravery and defence of the Colonel's home. Richard remained with the family on a good salary for only saying prayers with the servants each night, Alice married a tobacconist from Hexham, while Edward became the gamekeeper and received a *"fine, gold mounted gun"*. The Colonel later obtained a commission for Edward in a foot regiment but, after many adventures, he was shot through the shoulder at the battle of Fontenoy, retiring to a small farm north of the Border. Hogg states: *"I have often stood at his knee, and listened with wonder and amazement to his stories of battles and sieges, but none of them pleased me better than that of the Long Pack."*

❖❖❖❖❖❖❖

Haughton Castle, situated on the banks of the North Tyne opposite the village of Barrasford, is a fourteenth century fortified tower house, which, partly modernised, is inhabited today. This tale has its setting in the sixteenth century during the turbulent period of the Border Reivers and mosstroopers.

Sir John de Widdrington, a good, caring man, was Lord of Haughton at this time and he worked for peace, trying to suppress the unruly raiders. Lord Dacre of Gilsland, Warden of the Middle Marches, was the complete opposite to Sir John, and was suspected of taking bribes from chiefs of clans such as the Armstrongs, Scotts and Elliotts. Many of the raiders were causing more trouble than previously, using blackmail and extortion to terrify farmers. Lord Dacre was thought to associate with local characters such as Johnnie o' Gilnochie, Wat o' Harden and Kinmont Willie, who were all horse, sheep and cattle thieves.

Lord Dacre was also thought to be in love with Helen Armstrong, known as 'Dark-eyed Nellie', and the sister of the chief of the Armstrong clan.

The grievances of the local, honest landowners were brought to the attention of Sir John de Widdrington and he agreed to act as their envoy and put their case to the King. Sir John learned that the King's chief minister, Lord Cardinal Wolsey, was visiting York and arranged to meet him there, together with two local representatives.

The night before they set out, Sir John's men captured the chief of the Armstrong clan, brother of Helen, thieving cattle. Having thrown him in the dungeon, Sir John set off for York the next morning. After two days ride, the men were preparing to meet the Cardinal, when Sir John realised he still had the key to the dungeon in his pocket, and had left no instructions for food and water to be given to the prisoner.

Being a considerate man, and without seeing the Cardinal, he turned his horse and headed back North. He rode so hard that his horse dropped dead beneath him at Durham. He borrowed another and reached the castle within forty eight hours. Travel stained and exhausted, his first thought was for the prisoner. His servants replied that they had heard nothing from the chief of the clan for twenty four hours.

On entering the gloomy, foul-smelling dungeon, Armstrong was found to be dead, having gnawed at the flesh from his arm in his starvation. His features were horribly contorted and terrified all those present.

In the course of time, his ghost haunted the castle, his blood curdling shrieks echoing from the dungeon and reverberating throughout the rooms. None of the servants would remain in the castle and the family could get no rest from the agonising sound.

Eventually, the Rector of Simonburn exorcised the ghost using a black-lettered Bible which remained in the castle after the exorcism. The ghost was silenced until the Bible was taken to London for re-binding when he recommenced his desperate wailing. The Bible was quickly restored to the castle and the raider's spirit has remained silent.

❖❖❖❖❖❖❖

There continues to be an undiminished fascination with the Arthurian legend - was King Arthur indeed the son of Uther Pendragon, a British king with his famous Knights of the Round Table and founder of the brotherhood of chivalry? A strange old tradition persists that Arthur still exists, perhaps laid in a powerful spell, waiting release in order to deliver England from her troubles. The famous legend associated with Sewingshields illustrates this belief.

Almost a mile from Shield-on-the-Wall near to Carraw, between the Roman Wall and the military road, lies Sewingshields. A steep 'Shepherd's Pass' leads to the site of Sewingshields Castle of which nothing now remains above the ground. Hodgson's Northumberland history describes the area as *"a square, low, lumpy mass of ruins, overgrown with nettles."* In 1542 the castle was reported as belonging to John Heron of Chipchase and was even then *"very dilapidated."*

Stories and legends about the castle are woven into the history of the area, a barren moorland over which lingers a gloomy atmosphere of romance so that: *"undescribed sounds come a-swooning over hollow grounds"*. It is recorded that King Arthur, Queen Guinevere, their court of Lords and Ladies with their hounds, all lie in an enchanted sleep in a hall deep beneath the castle. So they will remain until someone, discovering their dilemma, first blows a bugle-horn which lies on a table near the hall entrance, and then with 'the sword of the stone', cuts a garter also lying there.

One day many years ago, a farmer or shepherd stumbled upon the subterranean passage leading to the hall, perhaps while in pursuit of something he had dropped. Pushing through piles of weeds, thistles and rubbish, he reached a vaulted passage infested with toads, lizards and bats. As he advanced a dim light ahead grew brighter, beckoning him on. Rounding a corner he suddenly entered a vast hall in the centre of which blazed a bright fire. Near to it, sitting and lying on thrones and couches were King Arthur, Queen Guinevere and all their court, while at their feet lay a pack of hounds. On the table close by were the horn, sword and garter needed to break the spell which held them enthralled.

The shepherd grasped the sword and drew it slowly from the rusty scabbard. To his amazement the King and his Court slowly stirred, stretched and began to open their eyes. Cutting the garter, the shepherd began to return the sword to its scabbard, but as he did so, the company sighed and sank down to sleep again. Before King Arthur closed his eyes, he gazed in anger at the unfortunate shepherd and said:

> *"O, woe betide that evil day*
> *On which this witless wight was born,*
> *Who drew the sword, the garter cut,*
> *But never blew the bugle-horn "*

The shepherd could never recall how he found his way back from the hall, he was in such a state of terror. Nor could he ever again find the entrance to the passage although he searched the site on many occasions.

So we may conjecture that King Arthur and his Queen and Court still sleep in enchantment, waiting their release.

All the area near to Housesteads on the Roman Wall is steeped in Arthurian legend. Two sandstone ridges to the north and a little to the west of Sewingshields are known as the 'King's and Queen's Crag' because of stories related to Arthur and Guinevere, and one of several basaltic columns among the nearby crags was called 'King Arthur's Chair'. To the north of Sewingshields an upright stone called 'Cumming's Cross' stands. Cumming was reputedly a northern chieftain who visited King Arthur at his castle, and was presented with a gold cup as a token of their lasting friendship. Alas that friendship only lasted until the King's sons heard of the visit. They set out after Cumming, killed him and buried him in the place where the stone stands.

Malory's *'Castle of Four Stones'* may be another clue, because of the four Roman stones from which Fourstones got its name. Arthur's Hill in Newcastle is yet another commemorative place-name. But it is at Bamburgh that we are surrounded with the full magical glamour of the Arthurian legends - for here 'perhaps' is Lancelot's own castle of 'Joyous Garde'. In this beautiful and haunting setting were enacted the two greatest love stories of all time : Tristram and Iseult, and Lancelot and Guinevere as portrayed in Wilfrid W. Gibson's verse:

"All in a golden haze,
I saw the gleaming towers of Joyous Garde
In splendour rise,
Tall, pinnacled, and white to my dream-laden eyes.
While thither, as in days of old,
Lancelot homeward came,
War-wearied, and yet wearier of the strife
Of love that tore his life;
Burning beneath the cold
Armour of steel, a never dying flame;
The fierce desire
Consuming honour's gold on the heart's altar fire.

And thither in great love he brought
The fugitives of love,
Isaud and Tristram fleeing from King Mark.
One day twixt dark and dark
These lovers, by fate caught
In love's bright web, dreamed with blue skies above,
Of love no tide
Of wavering life may part, or death's swift sea divide.

31

But Lancelot, in their bliss forlorn,
Fled from the laughter clear,
Of happy lovers, and love's silent noon;
All night beneath the moon
He strode, his spirit torn
For Guinevere. All night on Guinevere
He cried aloud
Unto the moonlit foam and every windy cloud."

After Lancelot's three years of wandering trying to forget Guinevere, he was betrayed to Arthur by Mordred and his brothers, and a trap was laid for him and Guinevere at Carlisle. Lancelot escaped, but Guinevere, condemned to death by fire, was *"led forth without Carlisle amid the weeping and wringing of hands of many lords and ladies."* Rescued by Lancelot and his friends amid a scene of great slaughter the lovers escaped to Joyous Garde where Lancelot *"kept her as a noble knight should do."*

Events followed, Arthur's siege of the castle, the reconciliation and Lancelot was banished overseas. When he returned in deepest sorrow at Arthur's death brought about by Mordred, Queen Guinevere had entered the abbey at Almebury, and Lancelot became a monk.

Before he died, he begged that his body might be buried at Joyous Garde, and Malory describes the account of this home-coming, together with Sir Ector's lament for the *"courtliest knight that ever bore a shield."*

The effigy of an unknown knight lies in Bamburgh church and has been traditionally called *'Lancelot du Lak.'*

❖❖❖❖❖❖❖

Many old Border castles, towers and peles have the reputation of being haunted. Bellister Castle on the South Tyne, close to Haltwhistle Station, is the setting for the legend of the 'Grey Man' - grey being the symbol for grief in folklore. Once a border stronghold, and in the possession of the Blenkinsopps until about 1470, it was described by Hutchinson in 1776 as *"a ragged and confused pile of mouldering walls, without any ornament or beauty."* Now only fragments of these outer walls remain as mute witness to the terrible events unfolded there.

An old travelling minstrel appeared late one evening at the entrance to Bellister and asked for shelter. Invited inside, he joined the Baron and the assembled company at their table in the Great Hall, and enjoyed food and wine. After the meal, as was the tradition, the minstrel played his harp and sang the old ballads of the Borders. The firelight flickered across his grizelled head, and as he sang, his features seemed to change, he looked younger, more straight and alert.

The evening wore on, wine was drunk, and as the Baron listened and dreamed he began to wonder whether the old minstrel was all he seemed. Might he not be an enemy spy or agent in disguise? In those far-off troubled times of Border feuds and raids, it was common for spies to infiltrate strongholds, perhaps dressed as servants, and so gain information about the occupants and their defences. The more the Baron pondered these thoughts, the more suspicious he became. He glared so fiercely and openly at him, that the poor old minstrel soon begged permission to retire for the night.

Some time later the Baron, by now thoroughly alarmed

by his thoughts, called his servants, and went to seek out the old man, determined to question him closely. But no trace could be found - the minstrel had vanished from the castle.

Quickly, the Baron ordered a search to be made outside, and released his bloodhounds who bounded swiftly into the woods. The defenceless old man was found hiding on the banks of the Tyne, but before the Baron reached the spot, the dogs savagely attacked and killed the minstrel.

In another version of the story, the old man was rescued before being killed by the dogs, and was then hanged from the branch of an ancient tree in front of the castle - known thereafter locally as 'The Hanging Tree'. In whatever manner he met his death, the old minstrel was brutally and horribly murdered, without any explanation being asked or given.

Whether the Baron's suspicions were well-founded or engendered by his own imagination would never now be known. The shadow of the 'Grey Man' became his constant companion, visible in light or dark, a cold unnerving presence which gave him no rest.

The Baron died early from his torments, but even after all his family were also extinct, and the castle had passed into other hands, the 'Grey Man' was still said to haunt the area.

At the end of the last century Bellister Castle finally fell into utter ruin. The last recorded appearance of the 'Grey Man' is said to have been one evening to a young man on his way to a nearby farm.

But perhaps the grey ghost still haunts the woods and river bank, unable to depart finally from the scene of his terrible death. Even today there are whispers of grey shadows seen among the hanging branches of the trees along the riverbank, and it is considered foolish to venture there alone after dark.

❖❖❖❖❖❖❖

Featherstone Castle, on the east bank of the South Tyne about three miles from Haltwhistle, enjoys a very picturesque setting, but the neighbouring woods have long been believed to be haunted. The horror of the events that happened there makes a sad, romantic and tragic story.

Hundreds of years ago, the Baron of Featherstone had a beautiful daughter named Abigail, whom he adored. She was to marry a nobleman of rank and fortune. But, unfortunately, the bridegroom was the Baron's choice. He had forbidden Abigail to meet again the man she truly loved.

Despite all her tearful protests, Abigail was married in the castle chapel by the Priest of Haltwhistle. Afterwards the full bridal party set out to 'ride the bounds' - that was to ride in procession around the entire boundary of the estate, as tradition demanded. On their return to the castle, a magnificent banquet would be held in their honour.

Abigail's lover had heard of this, and with a party of his friends, he was waiting in ambush in a little wood known as 'Pynkinsleugh'. His plan was to launch a surprise attack, rescue Abigail, and then they would make their escape together.

Back at the castle the feast was prepared and servants and minstrels waited with the Baron in the Great Hall to greet and serve the guests. Many hours passed without their return. The increasingly anxious Baron sent out men to search, but they could find no trace of the missing party. At last the servants were dismissed to bed, and only the Baron was left to keep a lonely vigil in the dimly lit Hall.

On the stroke of midnight he awoke from dozing to the sound of the castle drawbridge being lowered, and noises of horsemen in the courtyard. Almost in the same instance the bridal party filed silently into the Hall, and in dead silence took their places at the table. No-one spoke, not a single word.

Gazing in puzzlement at his guests, the Baron began to realise to his horror that the white and frozen faces of his daughter and friends belonged to their ghosts. With a terrible scream he fell to the floor in a faint, and as he did, the 'ghostly bridal party' vanished from sight.

According to the story, the poor Baron never recovered his speech, and remained paralysed for the rest of his life.

It was believed that when the bridal party was ambushed, a terrible fight had taken place, Abigail herself being accidently killed in the general confusion. No one survived the slaughter, and the blood from the dreadful carnage flowed into a hollow stone, which is known to this day as 'The Raven's Stone'.

Every year on the anniversary of the tragedy, the ghostly bridal party rides again through the woods near Featherstonehaugh. It is said that the sound of hoof-beats and the jingling of harness can be heard clearly. Strangely, although time has altered the landscape, the riders keep to their original route, passing straight through any walls or fences that now bar their way.

❖❖❖❖❖❖❖

Knaresdale Hall, about four miles south of Haltwhistle, once the ancient seat of the Pratt family, is reputed to have been haunted at one time.

The story tells how one of the Lairds of the Hall, (no dates are available for these strange happenings), a middle-aged man with no obvious physical attributes, gained parental permission to marry a lovely young girl of considerable wealth and beauty, against her wishes.

Constantly quarrelling with each other, the marriage was not a success. However, the girl gradually became less obviously dissatisfied and seemed at last to have accepted her fate. Unfortunately this was not as a result of a change of feelings towards her husband, but rather the attraction she felt towards a young nephew of the Laird's who had been brought up at the Hall with his sister.

The young wife and the handsome youth continued their illicit affair without discovery, until the boy's sister caught them embracing. Although the girl planned to keep silent in order to protect her brother, the lovers were fearful of her relating her story to the Laird and plotted to silence her.

The pair chose a particularly stormy night for the dreadful deed they had planned, the scene graphically described by William Pattison in the *'Local Historian's Tablebook'* : *"It was a night fitting to the deed: amid the thick and moonless gloom the storm raged wildly in the distant fells, and careering over the thick woods, came at last to the old Hall, and gathering strength and fed by mighty speats of rain, it fell on the aged walls and sturdy roof, and plashing on all sides, and driven by the wind with irresistible fury, the building rocked and groaned, and the casements flew in and opened, the rain entered, the house filled with hideous noises - the whistling of the blast and the clashing of many doors, which the evil night had bursten of their locks and hinges..."*

As the storm reached its height, the Laird was awoken by his wife, complaining about the noise of an open door banging at the rear of the house. She suggested that he send his niece to close it, although he was reluctant to do so, knowing he was more fitted to the task. However, anxious to please his wife, he remained at her side while the young girl, shivering in her cloak, obeyed.

She was about to close the door but her brother, lying in wait for her, seized his sister and plunged her into the overflowing waters of a nearby pond, holding her down until she was dead. He then threw her lifeless body into the depths of the pond.

Meanwhile, her uncle, concerned about her absence and feeling guilty at allowing the young girl to perform the task on such a dreadful night, was about to get up and look for her. His scheming wife, however, persuaded him that she had probably returned to her room and was sleeping.

Unaware of the plot to murder his niece, he resumed his sleep until woken by the sound of his dogs howling in the storm. He started up in bed and saw his niece standing by the fire, soaked through, wringing the water from her long hair. As he spoke to her, she vanished.

The girl's brother also mysteriously disappeared and was never heard of again. The young wife's guilt caused her to suffer 'brain fever' and during her ravings she disclosed some of the facts about the girl's disappearance. When the pond was dragged, the girl's body was found and shortly afterwards the guilty wife died - raving mad.

It is said that the girl's ghost was seen gliding from the rear door of the Hall to the pond each year on the anniversary of the tragedy, the old door would burst open of its own accord and crash on its creaking hinges.

❖❖❖❖❖❖❖

There are many records of the sightings of 'White Lady' ghosts, not just in Northumbria, but all over the country. It is the misty grey-white colour of the ectoplasm of which ghosts consist, that causes them to be described in this way. Three of the most well-known local appearances are related here, the first being : *'The White Lady of Blenkinsopp Castle'*.

Originally built in the early fourteenth century, the ruins of Blenkinsopp Castle stand on the River Tippalt, half-way between Haltwhistle and Greenhead. During the Middle Ages one of the castle's owners was Bryan de Blenkinsopp, a dark, handsome and brave warrior whose praises were sung by minstrels. His one failing was his greed and love of wealth, and although he was aware of this vice, and sought to control it, he was unable to overcome his longing for riches. Whilst attending the marriage of one of his friends, he was asked when he intended to take a wife, *"Never,"* said Sir Bryan, *"never shall that be, until I meet with a lady possessed of a chest of gold heavier than ten of my strongest men can carry into my castle."*

Ashamed of betraying such a secret, Sir Bryan left to fight in foreign wars, returning some years later with a beautiful wife. Her dark skin and strange ways attracted much gossip from the local people who thought she might be sent from the devil to steal Sir Bryan's soul. The most wondrous event, however, was that she brought with her a chest of treasure so heavy that twelve of Sir Bryan's men were needed to carry it into the castle - Sir Bryan had indeed fulfilled his vow!

In spite of their riches, however, the Lord and his wife were not happy together, and quarrelled constantly about the treasure which the bride would not surrender to her husband.

Finally, at dead of night, the lady ordered her servants to dig a great hole in the vaults of the castle in order to bury her riches where her husband could not hope to find them.

Sir Bryan, furious at her action and intent on punishing her, mysteriously left the castle and was never seen again. The deserted wife waited day after day for his return, eventually leaving the castle with her servants to disappear also. The gold lay hidden in the dungeons as the hauntings and strange happenings began.

Many local people claimed to have seen a white-robed figure, believed to be Sir Bryan's wife, mourning over the chest of gold which brought her such sorrow, and wandering through the partly ruined castle. A particular incident is recalled at the beginning of the nineteenth century.

Some of the more habitable rooms of the castle were occupied by workers on the estate, in this instance by a husband and wife, and their eight year old son. One night, several weeks after their move into the castle, their son woke up screaming and sobbing in an adjoining room. The parents ran to comfort him, but he was trembling with fear. He said he had seen a 'white lady' who sat at his bedside and *"cried sore"*, kissing the child and asking him to accompany her to where the treasure was buried, and she would make him a rich man.

The boy refused to go and as she stooped to lift him from the bed, he cried out, and she disappeared. The boy's ordeal was not over yet, the 'white lady' visited him on three consecutive nights, trying to persuade him to look for the gold. On the fourth night the parents moved the child into their own room and the apparition was not seen again.

Several years later a farmer began to clear away some of the rubble from the vaults in order to build cattle pens. The workmen were moving the accumulated rubbish of past centuries, when one of them uncovered the entrance to a tunnel. There was much speculation that it was the entrance to the 'Lady's Vault', and the news spread around the surrounding villages.

One man summoned the courage to enter the tunnel, taking a lantern with him into the dank gloom. The passage was narrow and he was unable to stand upright. Having walked a few paces, he descended a flight of steps and at the bottom found his way was barred by a wooden door, its hinges and bolts rusty and falling apart. At this point the passage turned sharply, leading to a flight of stairs. As the man ventured forth into the darkness to peer down the stairs, he opened his lantern to obtain more light and there was a rush of foul-smelling air, extinguishing the candle. He quickly returned to the vault with his story but the landowner showed no curiosity at his find, and ordered that the tunnel be closed and his own work continued.

At the end of the nineteenth century a lady came to stay at the village in Greenhead, about half a mile from the castle. She told the landlady of the inn that she had dreamt of a large chest of gold buried in the vaults of Blenkinsopp Castle, and that she was called upon to find it. She waited several weeks to gain permission to search the ruins of the castle, but it was not forthcoming as the owner was away from home. Eventually she left the district as mysteriously as she had arrived, empty handed.

Finally, Mr. William Pattison, a local historian visiting the castle in the 1840s, was amused to see some boys throwing stones into a hole they had broken in the wall near the entrance to the passage. They were listening to the hollow sounds of the stones as they rolled into the depths of the vault, totally unaware of the treasure reputed to have been buried there, and where many believe it remains to this day.

Our second 'white lady' appears in the old pele tower at Cresswell, a picturesque fishing village, overlooking Druridge Bay about six miles north of Newbiggin-by-the-Sea, and once the setting for this romantic but tragic legend.

A fine example of a medieval fortified tower house, Cresswell Tower was reputedly built by a baron of Cresswell, in the early Middle Ages. His beautiful, only daughter was in love with, and planned to marry, a brave young Danish prince who owned a small fort a few miles further north. Unfortunately, *"the course of true love did not run smooth"*, as the girl had three rash, impulsive brothers who hated her lover, and the idea that their Norman purity would be tainted by foreign blood when she married.

One day, when the prince was due to visit their sister, the brothers hid themselves in the long grass of the sand dunes, lying in wait for the unsuspecting Dane. Soon the prince rode into view, singing a love song, unaware of the danger which awaited him. Suddenly the brothers leapt from their hiding places, attacking the young lover with swords and spears, inflicting terrible wounds. As he fell from his horse, the prince's foot caught in one of the stirrups, and the horse, wounded and terrified, bolted towards the tower. The horribly injured, and by now, dead prince, hung in a macabre fashion from the dangling stirrups.

Waiting impatiently for her lover, the young girl had been looking for him from the top of the tower, and had witnessed these horrific events. The dreadful sight drove her instantly mad and she tore at her hair and cursed her headstrong brothers, predicting that they would all die a violent death within a year of their terrible deeds. Then the young girl, in her grief and madness, threw herself from the top of the pele tower, and fell, neck broken, on top of her dead lover.

The prediction concerning her murderous brothers came true. One brother was killed fighting the Scots, another was thrown from the saddle while out hunting, and justice was served as he too was dragged home by the stirrups, having broken his skull. The youngest brother perished at sea, drowned in a capsized boat. All died within a year of the dead lovers.

After these tragic events, the apparition of a lady, dressed in white garments, was said to haunt the tower. Every year on the anniversary of their brutal deaths, the 'white lady' is seen pacing back and forth on the top of the tower, as if waiting for her lost lover. Local people say that she looks to the north, shading her eyes with her hand impatient for his arrival. The sound of a horse's hooves is then heard, which ceases at the door of the tower, and a terrible wail of agony begins, dying away in an unearthly groan of pain and desperation.

Finally, we could not close this section without mentioning the 'White Lady' at the Lord Crewe Arms in the pretty village of Blanchland, situated in the Derwent Valley. An abbey was founded here in 1165 by the White Monks, from which the village got its name. Later, after the dissolution of the monasteries, the lands eventually passed to the Earls of Derwentwater, and finally, around 1623, to the Forsters of Bamburgh.

In 1701 Dorothy Forster, who had married Lord Crewe, Bishop of Durham in 1699, and her nephew, Thomas, who also had a sister called Dorothy, inherited the estate. By this time a manor house had been established, converted from the former kitchen and Prior's house, and this was later to become the present day 'Lord Crewe Arms'.

In 1715 Lady Crewe's nephew, Thomas Forster, together with the Earl of Derwentwater, took part in the Jacobite Rebellion, but, having surrendered at Preston before any battle could begin, he was taken to Newgate to await trial. His sister Dorothy, disguised herself as a servant and rode to London determined to rescue her brother.

Using duplicate keys, Forster made his escape from the governor's house and returned north with Dorothy. She concealed him in the Priest's Hole, a secret room in the kitchen chimney at the Blanchland Manor House, and later bought him a passage to France where he lived at the Pretender's court and later died.

Dorothy's ghost is said to haunt a wing of the hotel and can be heard opening and shutting doors. She is also said to re-arrange furniture and ornaments, and guests at the hotel claim to have felt the weight of her presence on their beds.

43

❖❖❖❖❖❖❖

On the central parapet of the gate tower which protected Tynemouth Priory from assault, a figure in a monk's garment stood and gazed intently out to sea. This was the time of the fearful Viking raids and Prior Olaf watched in dread for the red-brown sails of the serpent ships. Unknown to the brethren at Tynemouth, Olaf was himself a Dane, and in his youth he had been a follower of the Raven sign and the banner of Landwaster. Wounded in a raid into England and left for dead, he had been nursed back to health by a courageous band of monks. Later converted to their faith, he became a monk, and as spiritual leader of the priory, now worked tirelessly for the good of the local community. He shared their dread of the terrible raids which ravaged the coast, and felt acutely a dreadful conscience for his own past deeds.

As the wind had been easterly for several days, Olaf was filled with foreboding that a raid could be imminent. Descending to the chapel, he prayed long and earnestly at the shrine of Saint Oswyn, but even as he prayed, he heard a shout : *"They are coming, Holy Prior, God help us."* Calling the sub-prior to him, Olaf prepared to resist the onslaught of the enemy.

The Priory was splendidly situated for defence, being protected on three sides by moat, steep cliffs and the sea. The monks watched in terror from the walls as the enemy ships sailed up to the beach, and swarms of long haired men with swords and torches, uttering fearsome cries, came pouring up the cliffs. They were led by a young chief called 'Eric the Red'. Arriving at the gate, Eric demanded instant admittance and the surrender of all treasure, or else the place would be destroyed and everyone killed.

44

His demands being ignored, battle was immediately joined. Arrows hissed over the parapet, lighted torches were hurled against the gate, and a hail of stones were projected against the defences. The monks waited until the onslaught was at its height, then they launched a storm of stones and boiling lead. The heaviest of the stones crashed down onto Eric, driving his ribs deep into his lungs - a fatal blow. While the invaders paused in horror, the monks swiftly opened a small gate, and dragged the Danish leader into the Priory.

Shocked and disheartened by the capture and sure death of their chief, the raiders withdrew from Tynemouth. It is said that they descended on Shields and the surrounding countryside, burning and looting and killing, before returning to their ships and sailing southwards as the sun began to sink.

Inside the Priory it was realised that the young Dane was dead, and Olaf was summoned. Kneeling beside the body he murmured *"Eric"* again and again in silent anguish, his hands pressed against his heart and his white and ashen face hidden in the cowl of his habit - for in desperate grief he recognised his own brother. Giving orders to bury the body without delay, Olaf turned and, with faltering steps, walked towards the chapel where he sank to his knees in prayer.

Later, as the monks sang in praise and thanksgiving for their deliverance, it was realised that the Prior was absent. One of the monks hastened to the chapel, where he found Olaf still on his knees. Reaching out, he touched a cold, frozen hand - Prior Olaf had sought, and found, eternal rest. With tender care he was peacefully buried at Tynemouth, his grave, and that of Eric the Red, lovingly tended by the faithful monks. None ever remarked the resemblance which had been noticed between their beloved leader and the Dane.

Legend says that when the wind blows from the east, and the days are long and clear, the ghost of Prior Olaf still haunts the parapet of the Priory watching again for the sight of the demon raiders from the north.

❖❖❖❖❖❖❖

The scene of these hauntings is a house built in 1806 at Willington between North Shields and Wallsend, a fairly busy industrialised area even in the nineteenth century. Most of the events recorded took place between 1840-45 when the flour mill was the property of Messrs. Unthank and Procter.

There were various rumours of evil-doing by workers engaged in the building of the house, and that it was haunted by the ghost of someone who had been *"most foully murdered"* there. Witnesses reported seeing a bare-headed man dressed in a surplice at an upper window, he became known as 'Old Jeffrey'. A female figure was also seen, wearing a lavender coloured dress. She was most terrifying as she gazed out of eyeless sockets!

Two ladies, cousins of the owner Joseph Procter, had a horrifying experience when staying at the house. During the first night, they felt their bed rise up from the floor. On the second night the bed was violently shaken, and the bed curtains rapidly raised and closed. The next night, very bravely, they removed the bed curtains in order to see more clearly anything that happened. As they lay in bed, the misty figure of a woman appeared through the wall and floated above them, grinning down at them with a ghoulish relish...Not surprisingly, the sisters fled in terror, and the room was locked and never used again.

All these events received considerable press coverage, and there were many explanations offered to explain the spiritual manifestations. Finally, it was decided to conduct a *"scientifically recorded experiment"* at the house. A local man, Dr. Edward Drury, with the assistance of a chemist from North Shields, Thomas Hudson, arrived at the house on the evening of 3rd July 1840 to hold a vigil throughout the night.

Drury was armed with two pistols, and the two men sat on chairs on the third floor landing facing the rooms where most of the hauntings had taken place. By the light of their one flickering candle, they waited after the clock struck midnight to see what might occur...

Drury's own account of what happened later appeared in *'The Monthly Chronicles'*, he wrote:

"I took out my watch to check the time. It was 10 mins. to one. I saw the wardrobe door open and the figure of a female dressed in greyish garments appeared. Her head was bent forward, one hand pressed to her chest as if in pain, while with the other, the right, she pointed towards the floor. The figure advanced slowly to where my friend Hudson was sitting. I rushed towards it, yelling wildly, but instead of grasping it, I fell over Hudson, still dozing in his chair, and knew nothing more for about three hours."

Drury's story did coincide with the experiences of others who had stayed in the house. Hudson's own account of that night recalls that *"Drury's hair was standing on end, his face was the picture of horror. He fainted right away in my arms. There was nothing I could see in the room and the windows had not been opened."* This account by Hudson was first published in the *'Newcastle Weekly Chronicle'* on 20th Dec. 1884.

Several other people kept vigil at the house including : Mr. Thomas Davidson and Mr. John Ridley. They reported hearing sounds like a rivetter at work. Mr. J.D. Carr, Mr. Procter, Rev. Mr. Caldwell, and Rev. Mr. Robertson, all claimed to have heard mysterious sounds. How much was the product of their imagination, or the power of suggestion, it is impossible to tell. However, when the Procter family finally left the house, all the manifestations ceased.

❖❖❖❖❖❖❖

Although many of our tales feature hauntings of famous historic castles and houses, there have been just as many incidences in the homes of 'ordinary folk', as the following events from South Shields, originally related by William Brockie in his *'Legends and Superstitions of Durham'*, illustrate.

The 'old hall' in West Holborn, South Shields, once the residence of a wealthy ship owner, was later let out as flats or tenements, and was partly occupied by a public house. A lady lived there for quite some time and she, and her family heard and saw many strange things, including the mark of two bloody fingers and a thumb on one of the mantelpieces.

No amount of cleaning with any substance would remove the marks, they even reappeared through several coats of paint, and were regarded as the 'stains of murder', which were thought to be indelible. Many believed that the marks were those of a female victim *"of lawless depravity"* whose ghost was also seen from time to time.

One night as the lady lay reading, unable to sleep, the figure of a tall handsome lady in a white dress with a scarlet waistband, glided across the room. She came from a door which was permanently out of use, and crossing towards the window on the opposite wall, vanished.

Beneath the window sill where the apparition had disappeared was a hole, caused by a knot falling out of the wood, down which small articles were continuously falling. A member of the family hooked out various items, several dead beetles and other insects which may have infested graves. Later, the lady of the house wished she had removed the sill for closer inspection.

Other incidents also took place, including the apparition

of a soldier who was sometimes seen on the first floor landing. There was also one apartment in the house which was never entered, as it was believed to be a favourite haunt of supernatural beings. No tenant would rent the flat and it remained shut up for years, although there was no glass in the windows, the door remained firmly closed. *"What was in it beside the ghosts nobody knew or dared to investigate, for even to peep in to it through the key-hole would have needed more courage than most people possess, even if the spiders had not stretched their webs across it."* Occasionally strange noises were heard from behind the door, and many pondered what terrible murders or similar dreadful deeds had taken place there. *"Perhaps a hidden treasure lay under the floor, with the mouldering bones of murdered men."*

In another house in Thrift Street, South Shields, a servant girl was amazed to see an *"ancient ladye"* as she went down to the cellar one dark evening. The lady asked her to return the following night, but without her candle, and she would hear something to her advantage.

Venturing into the cellar the next evening, the girl decided to take the candle for safety, but the old lady informed her that if she had not brought the light, she would have told her *"such a tale."* The ghostly figure did agree to give the girl something for having had the courtesy to return that night.

Having been instructed to put her hand into a particular crack in the wall, the girl found the deeds to the house and a purse full of money. It was not known what became of the deeds, but the girl kept the money, left her job and became a *"grand lady"* for the rest of her life.

'Jack the Hammer' was a well-known personality in South Shields around the nineteenth century. He was a tall, good-looking old man, with a slight stoop, white hair, a Roman nose and high forehead. During his life, he travelled around the countryside mending pots and pans, leading a fairly ordinary life. Jack died, as he had lived, alone, and his body lay for some time before neighbours broke down the door of his house and discovered him.

It was unlikely that Jack had any hidden treasure, or even a guilty secret, but his spirit was not allowed to rest peacefully. His ghost appeared, usually during a gale when someone was lost at sea, and it would strike with a hammer at the end of his house, using tremendous power.

It was sometime before anyone would live in the old man's house, but eventually a man who was completely unafraid of ghosts was chosen by the landlord to clear the house's bad name.

A family rented a house in Stephenson Street, South Shields for a year, and were said to witness strange events. Shortly after moving into the house, the family were aware of weird disturbances, which were both puzzling and frightening. The patter of feet would be heard in a passage on the ground floor, but on investigation, there was no one to be seen. The sounds were heard both day and night, in all parts of the house.

Sleep was impossible in the lady's bedroom due to the incessant sound of a child's rattle which would circle the bed and could even be heard in the bed curtains. The rattle would seem close to her head, first on one side and then on the other, and then tiny feet would patter and run around the bed, accompanied by the sound of a child's cry or a woman sobbing.

The most distressing experience happened when the master of the house was away at sea. His wife took their small son to bed with her, fearful for his safety, when suddenly an inhuman voice was heard crying "*Weep! Weep! Weep!*", followed by gasps of breath, and then again, "*Weep! Weep! Weep!* ", a struggling for breath, and the same cry repeated a third time. Approaching the place where the sounds had come from, the mother, her terrified son clutching at her hand, asked several times what was wrong. The voices, obviously those of a sorrowing child and a distressed woman, were terrifying and heart-rending.

After a few days the lady decided to summon her courage and challenge the ghosts. As she called out for the intruders to reveal their identity, or cease disturbing the house, the sounds immediately stopped.

The ghosts revealed themselves only twice. Firstly, the clear figure of a child fell from the ceiling and vanished into the floor, and secondly, a child was seen running into a cupboard in a room at the top of the house. No matter how often the cupboard door was closed, it would open itself, even before the lady left the room. This particular place became the centre of the hauntings and the sound of creaking shoes pacing back and forth, were heard, day and night.

After a year the family were thankful to be leaving the house. Five or six years later, a new buyer was carrying out alterations, and the skeleton of a child was discovered under the floorboards close to the cupboard door. Some years before the house had been occupied by a disagreeable man who was on intimate terms with his female servant. Local people drew their own conclusions from this, and it may be assumed that at one time a child died tragically in what was thought to be an 'ordinary' house.

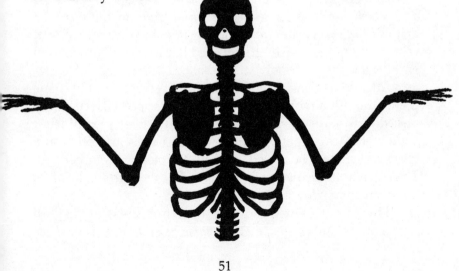

❖❖❖❖❖❖❖

An incident recorded by John Wesley in his journal concerns a young woman, Elizabeth Hobson, of Sunderland. She had experienced a number of ghostly encounters including having had, on two occasions, visions of her brothers at the point of death, only to discover that they were actually dying some distance from home. Also, during an illness the ghost of an uncle appeared before her, accompanied by music and singing which faded away after each visit.

Not so pleasant, and the main subject of Wesley's recordings, was the appearance of her departed grandfather, John Hobson, who, having died 14 years previously, returned to torture and torment her. Having led a *"wicked"* life, he left his house in Sunderland to Elizabeth's brother, John, which she then inherited in 1762. At this time it was occupied by two aunts who refused to leave, and despite legal action, Elizabeth gave up her efforts to regain the property.

Her grandfather's ghost, however, was more persistent and a few nights after her decision to give up the fight, he appeared before her and addressed her sternly about relinquishing the house. He ordered her to go to Durham and employ a lawyer to resolve the problem.

After some consideration Elizabeth decided not to pursue the matter but a month later the ghost re-appeared, pacing up and down before her for half an hour. Her grandfather continued these nightly visits for three weeks and often in a *"paroxism of rage"* he seized and tore the clothes from her bed. These terrifying experiences brought Elizabeth to the brink of a nervous breakdown.

The ghost continued to haunt her until at last, in desperation, she cried *"In God's name, why do you torment me*

thus? You know it is impossible for me to go to Durham now."
Continuing, she asked her grandfather if he was happy but he replied that her question was a bad one and she must do better in her life than he had done in his. Elizabeth spoke of the Lord and his mercy but this made the ghost very angry and, forbidding her to mention God's name, it disappeared in a flash of flame.

When she had recovered, Elizabeth visited Durham to consult a Mr. Hugil and asked him to deal with the property in Sunderland. The ghost re-appeared shortly afterwards insisting that the lawyer was not acting correctly, having only written one letter to the aunts.

Exasperated, Elizabeth asked her grandfather why he didn't haunt the aunts but he replied that he did not have the power to intimidate them and could not leave his grandaughter alone until the matter was resolved.

She continued to endure pressure from the apparition for seven months from December 1767 until the following July when she finally gained possession of the house. Following the day of the settlement, Elizabeth's grandfather appeared and asked her to meet him at Boylden Hill at midnight where he would offer an explanation regarding his strange behaviour.

Prior to the meeting, some of Elizabeth's friends met and prayed with her and six decided to accompany her to Boylden Hill. They waited a little distance from the meeting place but later claimed not to see anything.

The ghost appeared before Elizabeth and threatened that he would haunt and persecute her to the end of her days if she revealed to anyone what he was about to say.

She kept her promise and we must assume that she was then left in peace. John Wesley seems to have been impressed by the story and believed her to be religious and sincere. We cannot tell if these strange happenings actually occurred or whether Elizabeth was merely seeking attention.

❖❖❖❖❖❖❖

"Hush a ba! babby! be;
For Sharp and Walker killed thou and me"

\- Nursery Rhyme

The idea of the ghost of a victim returning to denounce its murderer, is not a new one. Warnings or advice have often been given from the 'other side', particularly when violence has taken place. This is one such incident which took place in the seventeenth century near Chester-le-Street, based on a version of the story in *'The History of Durham'* by John Surtees.

John Grahame, a miller from Lumley, near Chester-le-Street, would not have called himself a superstitious man, but events which took place at his mill in the early 1630's caused him to question his beliefs.

The miller was a happy, contented man with few worries, who laughed at people's fear of the supernatural, at a time when belief in witches, fairies and the like was rampant. At the time in question, when the harvest had been gathered in, he arrived earlier at his mill, staying until after dark.

Imagine him then, happy at his work as the mill wheel turned and the golden grain flowed in the light of the candle, which lent the white sacks of grain an eerie glow, as they lay like a ghostly regiment ready for inspection. The miller was unaware of these ghostly overtones until there was a change in the atmosphere and his flesh crept as he felt his blood run cold.

There, standing before him, was a woman with blood streaming from her head, staining her wild, tangled hair a deep crimson. She had five terrible wounds in her head, the blood continually gushing forth.

"She looked at him with a fixed, stony, lifeless stare that for a moment froze the current of his blood."

Summoning all his courage, the miller asked how she had received such terrible injuries. The girl told him that she was Anne Walker, a relative of his neighbour, John Walker, who had seduced her, resulting in pregnancy. Anxious to be rid of her, he then persuaded his accomplice, Mark Sharp, a pitman from Lancashire, to take her away where Anne believed she would be looked after until she could return to Walker.

Sharp, however, murdered her, inflicting the five wounds to her head with a miner's pick, and throwing her body into a pit. Unable to wash the stains from his blood-soaked shoes and stockings, he hid them, together with the pick, under a bank.

The mutilated girl begged the miller to reveal the truth about the dreadful deed, and disappeared.

Grahame, now terrified, hurried home to his wife but could not bring himself to tell her about the terrible apparition, unable to confess the fear he had experienced. The miller continued at his work as usual but no longer stayed late at the mill, which delighted his wife although she could not guess at his reasons.

However, one night he stayed a little longer at the mill and once again the distraught figure appeared. Having previously begged for help, the girl now assumed a commanding presence, warning him to reveal the murder or suffer further apparitions.

Grahame was still reluctant to go to the magistrate - his friends would think he was out of his mind. He retained his silence but became moody and began to lose weight, prompting enquiries from friends and relatives.

Finally, whilst walking in his garden on St. Thomas' Eve, before Christmas, the ghost appeared again before him. More threatening than the previous times, she extracted a promise from Grahame that he would visit the magistrate the next day and reveal the facts of her brutal murder.

He kept his promise and the following day a search was made of the pit where the girl's mutilated body was subsequently found. A further search revealed the hidden pick and the shoes and stockings. John Walker and Mark Sharp were arrested and the local people were able to piece together Anne's story.

Walker, an unpleasant man who abused his wife, had never been liked by his neighbours who verified that Anne Walker had disappeared very suddenly after her arrival as supposed housekeeper. They had suspected Walker as the father of her child, although she had not revealed his identity.

The trial took place in August 1631 before Judge Davenport and lasted only one day. One witness, a Mr. Fairhair, stated that throughout the trial he could see the likeness of a child on Walker's shoulders and the Judge, deeply disturbed, gave the sentence that same night. Walker and Sharp were condemned to death and subsequently executed.

The ghost was seen no more but the spot where the murder took place, a ravine in the Old Mill Wood, was known afterwards, locally, as 'Sharp and Walker's Gill'.

Pickax & Shovel

THE LAMBTON WORM

❖❖❖❖❖❖❖

The Lambton Worm, written about extensively in both prose and verse, must be one of the best known of our local legends. 'Worm' is a misleading term for the monstrous creature which rose from the River Wear. The word is taken, in fact, from the old Norse word 'ormr', meaning a serpent or dragon.

The Lambton family name can be traced back for many generations, the original Lambton Castle being pulled down in 1797, and replaced by the present mansion which stands on the north bank of the River Wear. These particular events are thought to have taken place in the thirteenth century, as the young heir was known to have fought in the Crusades.

John Lambton, the remaining heir to Lambton Castle, was, in his youth, wild, impulsive and bad mannered and broke all the rules, especially by going fishing on Sundays instead of attending Church. One particular Sunday he was fishing in the Wear, not far from the castle, when he eventually felt something tugging at his line. Hoping for a fine salmon, he was bitterly disappointed to find an ugly worm on the end of the hook. Disgusted at its horrible appearance, he immediately threw it down a nearby well.

Having just cast his line again, a stranger passed by, asking *"What sport?"*, to which John Lambton replied, *"I think I've just caught the Devil himself"*, and showed the man the creature he had flung into the well. It was indeed an ugly sight, resembling an eel, but having nine holes on each side of its mouth. As he left, the stranger remarked that he had never seen *"the like of it"* and that no good would come of it.

The Worm was, therefore, left in the well and, according to the well-known song, *"growed and growed"*, until it became too big and emerged to find another home. By day the serpent coiled up on a rock in the River Wear, and at night twined itself around the base of a nearby hill, growing in length, until it eventually was wrapped three times around the mound. The monster terrorised the countryside devouring sheep and lambs, sucking cows' milk, uprooting crops and causing great distress and hardship to the local peasants. Having laid waste to the land north of the river, it crossed the stream and advanced towards Lambton Hall, where Lord Lambton now lived alone, in grief and sorrow. His son, John, having repented his sins, had left to fight in the Holy Wars.

The Lord summoned his steward, a man of *"great age and experience"*, to find a solution to rid them of the terrible monster. The steward could only suggest that they keep the creature at bay by filling a trough with milk everyday to satisfy the serpent's appetite. It took the yield of nine cows to fill the trough each night, but the Worm came to drink and seemed content to curl up and sleep on the rock by day, and around the hill at night. If a peasant dared to steal a drop of milk from the trough, the Worm knew when it had been robbed and flew into a fierce rage, lashing its tail around the trees in the park and uprooting them.

Many gallant knights travelled to Lambton in an attempt to slay the monster, but none succeeded. Often it was severed in half but miraculously the parts came together again and it seemed to suffer no weakness.

Eventually, John Lambton returned home, now a fine brave man, and heard of the trouble for which he felt responsible. He pledged to rid his father of the terror and consulted a witch, or 'sibyl' who lived nearby. He was told that in order to slay the serpent he must stand on the beast's rock in the middle of the river, wearing his best suit of armour, studded with spears, so that when the Worm tried to crush him, it would be cut to pieces. A condition of this advice was that if he was successful in killing the Worm, he should then kill the first living thing he met, otherwise the next nine generations of the Lords of Lambton would not die in their beds.

Having equipped himself with the necessary armour, and a sharp sword, he took up his stand on the rock and waited for the Worm to approach its daily resting place. In due course the creature slithered into view, and the knight, eager to start the fight, struck the Worm a terrible blow to the head. In a dreadful rage, the Worm began to coil itself around Lambton's body, and as it wrapped itself more tightly to him, he began to see the value of the witch's advice. The Worm was being cut to pieces, its self-inflicted wounds causing the stream to run red with blood. As its strength was sapped, the brave knight was able to cut the serpent into two, the pieces being swiftly carried away by the force of the current in the stream. At last - the Lambton Worm was dead!

John Lambton had agreed to blow a bugle to signal to his father that the deed was accomplished. Lord Lambton could then send one of his favourite hounds to be the first living thing his son encountered after killing the Worm, thus fulfilling the witch's condition. However, hearing the signal, the old man was so relieved that he rushed forward to embrace his son. John Lambton could not bear to raise his sword against his own father and blew again on the bugle. This time it summoned the hound, and, as it approached, John plunged his sword into its heart.

However, his action was in vain and, the vow broken, the curse of the Lambton's was upon them. This prophecy did, in fact, partially come true. John Lambton's son was drowned, two other heirs died in battle, and the ninth of the generations, Henry Lambton, died in his carriage crossing Lambton Bridge.

❖❖❖❖❖❖❖

In the past, it was the custom for the lead miners of Allendale and Weardale to receive a certain amount of money each month to cover expenses, and, at the end of each year, a general settlement would take place between the employers and the workers. This particular day was known as 'Pay', and it would attract an influx of travellers and tradesmen from neighboroughing districts, knowing that there would be plenty of money around to settle bills.

The travellers would often engage a guide to help them across the unknown tracks and bridle paths in such a wild, desolate and mountainous part of the country. The threat of attacks from highwaymen was a constant worry.

In the middle of the eighteenth century, a traveller was collecting debts at Alston, Nenthead and Allendale, and arrived in Weardale where he paid and dismissed his guides, hoping to engage others to assist him through Teesdale.

Completing his business, he found it impossible to hire any guides for a few days and not wishing to waste time, set off alone. The road was a poor one, suitable only for carts, and was enclosed by high banks covered with tall trees, cut out here and there to allow other vehicles to pass. Torrents of water frequently rose up at one side and crossed the stony road, forming deep pools over which no bridges were built.

Alone in a strange place, on a dark road, in charge of a large sum of money, the man saw few other travellers. Somewhat frightened, he pressed on anxiously into the night. Having been seen by at least one or two travellers, he disappeared without trace, after reaching a place called Park-House Pasture.

At midnight, the owner of an isolated farm at the end of

this field was awoken by loud screams of agony and despair, together with the sound of a horse's hooves trampling back and forth. Horrified, but wanting to investigate, the old man was restrained by his wife and daughter until morning.

At daybreak the farmer closely inspected the wet and marshy field; it bore the deep marks of a horse's hooves, and impressions made by human feet. Nearby, access to a narrow lane was blocked by two gates, through which anyone wishing to leave the field would have had to pass. On further investigation, however, the old man found that the gates had been tied together and made secure to prevent anyone from escaping.

News of the missing traveller spread fast and suspicion finally rested on three men who had kept a horse concealed for many days behind some curtains. They had also been seen forcing a horse down an old, unworked pit. Adding further to their guilt, the men suddenly became very rich, possibly as a result of stealing the traveller's money.

Exhaustive enquiries were made by the missing man's friends and relatives, but no real evidence could be found to use against the suspects. Many years later, however, at the beginning of the nineteenth century, improvements were made to the roads, including one which was to cut through the Park-House Pasture. As excavations were carried out the skeleton of a man was discovered buried in an upright position, thus reviving the legend of the missing traveller.

Local people claim that at dead of night, a phantom horse, with a bleeding rider, jumps over the field and disappears into an old quarry where the hideous relics were found.

A BASINFUL O' GEORDIE
by Dorfy
A selection of humorous Tyneside readings in dialect.

THE BODY IN THE BANK: famous Northern murders
Retold by Sandhill Press
A fascinating collection of murders, trials and subsequent harsh punishments which took place in our northern towns & countryside.

CUSTOMS & TRADITIONS OF NORTHUMBRIA
Retold by Sandhill Press
Customs and traditions associated with ceremonies, seasons and times of the year, leisure and work activities are all investigated.

THE GREAT GUNMAKER: the life of Lord Armstrong
by David Dougan
A fascinating biography of the north's famous armaments manufacturer.

IN AND AROUND
ALNWICK...MORPETH...ROTHBURY...WARKWORTH
by Ian Smith
First in a new series in which Ian explores Northumberland's towns, villages and their rivers. Written in the author's inimitable style, the book also includes Ian's own line drawings and maps.

THE LAST YEARS OF A FRONTIER
by D.L.W. Tough
A history of the Borders during the turbulent times of Elizabeth I.

MAD DOGS AND CYCLISTS : on two wheels through Northumbria
by Chris Rooney
Rich lyrical prose and humorous anecdote are combined to relate the joys of cycling.

MEDIEVAL CASTLES, TOWERS, PELES & BASTLES
OF NORTHUMBERLAND
by T.H. Rowland
A reprint of this comprehensive guide to the many castles and Border strongholds which form part of Northumbria's rich, often troubled history.

MYTH AND MAGIC OF NORTHUMBRIA
Retold by Sandhill Press
*Wizards and witches, fairies and sprites, charms and spells -
a retelling of strange happenings from Northumbria's folklore.*

NORTHUMBRIA IN PICTURES
*A new revised edition of our successful colour souvenir guide-
40 superb colour photographs and accompanying text.*

NORTHUMBRIAN COASTLINE
by Ian Smith
*A walker's guide from Berwick upon Tweed to North Shields printed in the
author's own handwriting & including his many line drawings and maps.*

THE NORTHUMBRIAN PUB : an architectural history
by Lynn F. Pearson
A social and architectural history of our north eastern pubs.

ROGUES & REIVERS OF THE NORTH COUNTRY
Retold by Sandhill Press
Tales of highwaymen, smugglers, bodysnatchers & the Border Reivers.

UPPER COQUETDALE
by David Dippie Dixon
*Northumberland : its history, traditions, folklore and scenery.
Originally published in 1903 - a special limited numbered edition.*

VICTORIAN & EDWARDIAN NORTHUMBRIA
FROM OLD PHOTOGRAPHS
By J.W. Thompson & D. Bond

WARKWORTH
by Ian Smith
A charming guide to this unique Northumbrian village.

YORKSHIRE COASTLINE
by Ian Smith
*A follow up to the highly successful 'Northumbrian Coastline', this second
guide covers the coast from the RiverTees to Bridlington.*